什么是税

How We Organize Ourselves | Non-Fiction Series

Copyright © 2022 by Level Learning, INC. and Washington Yu Ying PCS™
Original and Edited Text Copyright © 2022 by Washington Yu Ying PCS™

All rights reserved. No part of this book in whole or part may be reproduced without written permission from the publisher.

Published by Level Learning, INC.
Content Contributors:
Washington Yu Ying PCS™ - Qianyi (Shirley) Zhang, Pearl Zao He You
Level Learning - Jingyao Qi

Illustrations by: Josh Taira

Leveling classification based on Level Learning standard.
For full description, visit www.levellearning.com

ISBN 978-1-64040-121-1
Simplified Chinese Edition

About Level Learning:

Level Learning provides a literacy focused curriculum specifically designed for K-12 Chinese as a Second Language classrooms. Our program offers 20 levels of specific and detailed objectives, leveled texts and passages, mastery-based online assessment, and analytics to enable data-driven instruction. Level Learning reading curriculum for both literature and informational text emphasize grammar and comprehension skills to help teachers develop confident and independent Chinese language readers. The non-fiction series of books are specifically designed to support our informational text course based on multiple national standards. To learn more about our entire offering, visit www.levellearning.com.

About Washington Yu Ying PCS™:

Washington Yu Ying PCS is a Mandarin English dual language immersion International Baccalaureate (IB) World school. Yu Ying's mission is to inspire and prepare young people to create a better world by challenging them to reach their full potential in a nurturing Chinese/English educational environment. Yu Ying's comprehensive IB, dual immersion curriculum equips students with global competencies for success in the real world. As a leader in immersion education, Yu Ying is determined to advance Chinese language programs and global citizenry education by helping other schools create and strengthen their Chinese programs. For more information, email: products@washingtonyuying.org

你喜欢去公园玩或是去图书馆看书吗？你去过国家公园旅行或者露营吗？你看过美国国庆日夜晚美丽的烟花吗？

你有没有想过，为什么公园总是那么干净整洁？为什么图书馆里总有新的图书？为什么公立学校不用交学费？那些美丽的烟花又是怎么来的？这些公共服务的费用都是来自人们交的税。

在美国，税收是政府向人们收取的费用，主要用于公共服务。政府的税收关系到人们日常生活的方方面面。

除了公园、图书馆等公共设施以外，道路交通的修建和维修也离不开税收。另外，政府的税收还要负责军队和各个政府机构的开支，比如消防局、警察局等。

RECEIPT
THANK YOU

SODA 汽水	$5.95
POTATO CHIPS 薯片	$2.99
CANDY 糖果	$1.89
4 SANDWICHES 4个三明治	$18.75
10 GALLONS OF GAS 10加仑汽油	$31.00
SUBTOTAL 小计	$60.58
STATE SALES TAX 州消费税	$4.24
TOTAL 总计	$64.82

美国大部分州都有消费税。仔细看一看你买东西的账单，在账单的最后一行你会看到你交了多少消费税。不同的州，消费税也不同。人们工作的收入需要交所得税。所得税会根据收入的高低而不同。

税的种类很多。除了消费税和所得税，还有关税、营业税、房产税等等。不仅个人需要交税，公司和团体也是要交税的。如果你中了彩票，或者得到一大笔遗产或财产，这些钱也都是要交税的哦！

APRIL
四月

15

TAX DAY
报税日

每年4月15日左右是美国的"报税日"。税务局(IRS)会根据公司或个人一年的收入和已经交的税,来决定是退还一部分税给你,还是需要你补交一些税。你有没有注意到,人们在每年的4月总是忙忙碌碌的,那是因为大家都在忙着报税呀!

Glossary

	Pinyin	English Definition
图书馆	tú shū guǎn	library
露营	lù yíng	camping
国庆日	guó qìng rì	National Day (in the U.S., July 4th is our Independence Day)
烟花	yān huā	fireworks
干净	gān jìng	clean
整洁	zhěng jié	neat
公立	gōng lì	public
交	jiāo	to pay
学费	xué fèi	tuition
公共	gōng gòng	public, common
服务	fú wù	service
税收	shuì shōu	taxation
政府	zhèng fǔ	government
收取	shōu qǔ	to collect
费用	fèi yòng	fee

	Pinyin	English Definition
主要	zhǔ yào	main, primary
用于	yòng yú	use for
方方面面	fāng fāng miàn miàn	all aspects
设施	shè shī	facility
道路	dào lù	road
交通	jiāo tōng	connection
修建	xiū jiàn	to build
维修	wéi xiū	to fix, to maintain
负责	fù zé	responsible
军队	jūn duì	military
机构	jī gòu	organization
开支	kāi zhī	spending
消防局	xiāo fáng jú	fire station
警察局	jǐng chá jú	police station
消费税	xiāo fèi shuì	sales tax

Glossary

	Pinyin	English Definition
仔细	zǐ xì	carefully
账单	zhàng dān	bill
所得税	suǒ dé shuì	income tax
随着	suí zhe	following
收入	shōu rù	income
关税	guān shuì	custom tax
营业税	yíng yè shuì	business tax
房产税	fáng chǎn shuì	estate tax
公司	gōng sī	company
团体	tuán tǐ	group
彩票	cǎi piào	lottery
遗产	yí chǎn	inheritance
财产	cái chǎn	property, estate
报	bào	report
根据	gēn jù	according to

	Pinyin	English Definition
决定	jué dìng	to decide
退还	tuì huán	to refund
补交	bǔ jiāo	to make up payment
忙忙碌碌	máng máng lù lù	busy

www.ingramcontent.com/pod-product-compliance
Lightning Source LLC
Chambersburg PA
CBHW041224070526
44584CB00001B/81